Halina Goldstein

# Love Songs
## Spiritual Poetry

Copyright © Halina Goldstein 2021
All Rights Reserved

Edited by: Frances Bryant-Scott
Cover art: Laura Cassini
Cover design: June Design
Published by: BoD – Books on Demand, Copenhagen, Denmark
Printed by: BoD – Books on Demand, Norderstedt, Germany

1st edition
ISBN: 9788743028642

No part of this publication may be reproduced in any form or by any means, including scanning, photocopying, or otherwise without prior written permission of the copyright holder

# Contents

Loving ........................................................................................... 8
I Am An Ocean Of Love ............................................................. 9
Playfulness ................................................................................. 10
The Sunset ................................................................................. 11
The Heron .................................................................................. 12
The One ..................................................................................... 13
Waiting ....................................................................................... 14
Being Lived ................................................................................ 15
And The Moment Passes .......................................................... 16
This will pass too ...................................................................... 18
If only I knew ............................................................................ 19
Living ......................................................................................... 20
My wings long ........................................................................... 21
Evening ...................................................................................... 22
Rainbow ..................................................................................... 24
Why ............................................................................................ 25
Resistance speaking ................................................................... 26
How to untie a Gordian knot ................................................... 27
Enough ....................................................................................... 28
This is the way .......................................................................... 29
The seed ..................................................................................... 30
The gate is closing behind me ................................................. 31

| | |
|---|---|
| Loosening the grip | 32 |
| Opening | 33 |
| The only home | 34 |
| The prodigal daughter | 35 |
| Loving What Is | 36 |
| Wait | 37 |
| It's not what it looks like | 38 |
| The destination | 39 |
| Arrivals | 40 |
| It is happening | 41 |
| Words | 42 |
| The answer | 43 |
| Dying | 44 |
| The cup | 45 |
| The agreement | 46 |
| My soul | 47 |
| I am love | 48 |
| Thank you | 50 |
| Gratitude | 52 |
| About the author | 54 |
| Other books by Halina | 55 |

# Loving

You have crossed my path
A stranger I recognized
Yet do not know

You changed my world
So it seemed
And yet
As it turns out
With you or without you
It is the loving itself
That changes the world

# I Am An Ocean Of Love

I am an ocean of love
I may be calling you
But it is for you to choose
The place and the time
Of your arrival
I offer my waves to you
But it is for you to choose
Your way
Surf me
Swim me or
Sail me
I will carry you home
Dive into me or
Drown and be one with me
I will embrace you
For all time
I am an ocean of love
Trust me

# Playfulness

I am a piece of art
Making itself

# The Sunset

I don't have to stay here all evening
After all
This is not the first sunset I have ever seen
And yet
After all
It is

# The Heron

You see me
Wings spread
But not for flying
Only waiting
But then
At the slightest unexpected sound
Or movement
Taking flight after all
And then
Coming back
To guard my waiting place

Again and again
This is all you see
Not the real life that I live
The wild life of the One

# The One

This is the nowhere land
The place where I am waiting
For the bursting and the birthing

Behind the closed gates
The point of no return
And no directions
An invitation card
With nothing written on it

While I'm here
I can make whatever I want of it
Breathe it
Drink it

And then

I am
I am being her and him and this
And you
I am becoming you
The One

# Waiting

The notes on the table
The candle burning
You will never come back
Because
You have never left me

# Being Lived

My heart is so happy
And yet so close to aching

As I remember
I forget
As I know I am love
I long for love
As I sink into presence
I think myself away

What sweet foolishness
And how little I can do about it

These waves from the sea
Rise and fall

Somewhere between them
I can feel
How I am being lived

# And The Moment Passes

A radio playing in a room abandoned
I am vibrating
Taut between the walls of my body
And once again wondering
How come it's so

Yet nothing is missing
In the joy of me alone

And only then
My darling
You come to me

You are you
And it's not what I have been imagining
It's beautiful in a different way
And it's opening between us
For one short moment in time

You had nowhere to go
I wasn't there to receive you

But now the magic can happen
That we will not speak of
And not even see in the same way

And the moment passes

# This will pass too

A dark cloud is here

I know
All it takes is more wind and this will pass too
Like a sailboat disappearing behind the horizon

This will pass too
So they say
The truth is
That the wind that cleared the sky
Is bringing another boat
And another cloud

How to live this life
Of hopes and disappointments
How to live this life
Of love and not be longing
How to be the welcoming
Of the everchanging skies

# If only I knew

The grace of me
Alone and moving
Around my spacious home

There is such sweet and blind beauty
To me missing
The you that I imagined you to be

# Living

This apartment where I have lived for ten years
Feels just like the hotel I visited last month
It's nice to be here
I appreciate the way it is arranged

The hotel I will visit next month
Will feel like home as much as this apartment
Familiar and unfamiliar

This place is as good a place to die as any other
Or to be born for that matter

It never ends
It never begins
It just feels that way

# My wings long

My wings long for a bigger sky
I tremble with impatience
But my feet
My strong bird feet
Cling to the black nest that holds me
This tree that holds its strength like an old woman
This landscape that I know so well
This safe place

I wish I was something else

Something within me whispers
"I am more than they told me about me"
"I am more"

And still I don't know
Whether I want to stay
Or fly

# Evening

You have been waiting an eternity
But I couldn't make it in time
My time was reserved
For more important tasks

Yet here we are
Am I ready?

I am not sure
Of anything
Yet I promise
I swear on this evening sky
Bringing its darker blue towards us

Soon

How futile and fragile
My body feels
This hand
This writing
This smile on my face

How I love the imperfection of living
So rich in this moment

And the short glimpse of knowing
That all the worldly obligations and tribulations
Are nothing
Cause nothing compares to you
My soul

I love you
Is it you saying it
Or is it me?

Like a rock
Permeated by light
And then dissolving
In front of our eyes
I convinced myself
I was building my grand future

Until the divine laughter
Sounded everywhere

Wake up!
Take it or leave it
Make it or shake it
What else is there to do

Meanwhile
The evening blue gets deeper
In a transparent kind of way

Un-dark as much as dark

# Rainbow

Between tears and light
I am being
Stretched and arched

I am a rainbow

# Why

In a split of a moment
The past against the future

Why am I still reasoning
Against love?

# Resistance speaking

No
It's not personal
I just don't want you to go there
And no
I'm not going to get out of your way
I will stand here
Until you ask me what I want
Then, I will shrug

I will stand here
Right in front of you

I am a messenger
Ask for the message

You have to ask me first

You have to look me in the eye
And listen

After that it's up to you
My work is done
We can part our ways
As friends

# How to untie a Gordian knot

Wait
Wait until you can see
The ropes loosening
And falling to the ground
Like feathers

# Enough

I am a fireman
Cleaning my suit with a hose
And later my body
I have put all the fires out
There's nothing I want anymore

I lie down to rest
My arms under my head
Looking at the ceiling
Breathing
This is good
This is enough

My heart disagrees

One soft touch of an angel wing
Melts all my defenses

# This is the way

Now that I am not here
My eyes see wonders everywhere

Oh the fullness of it
When life just lives itself without me
Through my body and senses and joy
And no unnecessary thoughts
To mislead and misread reality

I am demolishing myself and the original wound
And everything that followed

And then I lie down on the ground
Like red dust and shadows
Nothing more
The end of myself

Here is the border
Now is the time to cross it
This is the way

# The seed

I am a wind blowing through the empty streets in winter's dusk
Finding my peace at the gates of the sacred woods
Where the trees are dry cold and bare
But still standing

Like we are
Unknowingly together
Even as we seem apart

I forget who I am in this world
I am creating all this in my mind
This tragicomic journey
This swinging from one side to the other
In a never lasting balance
Losing myself in the past
I never lived for real

I am a wind carrying the seed of the future
Promising nothing but itself and freedom
Nothing but joy

# The gate is closing behind me

I hardly moved through the gate
Hardly knew that this was what was happening
And already I feel the heavy doors closing behind me
Pushing me forward this way

There is no turning back now

# Loosening the grip

I tried to hold on to this solid cliff
Like a place to hide and stay
But even there you found me
Your waves loosened my grip
Your waters washed me down
I am becoming a current in your ocean
And so is the cliff
It crumbles away and apart
It falls and disappears
Into you

# Opening

It is the unclinging
And the dying out
That does it for me

Gently
My soul opens
What is left of me
Persistent
Waiting
A lover
That knows me
More deeply than I know myself
Assuring me

There is no hurry
And no retreat

# The only home

I am a single yurt in a Mongolian desert
All I want is to feel the winds of it
No matter how harsh
These are the winds of God

# The prodigal daughter

I took a lifetime to find my way back
You don't seem to hold it against me
That I am late

So late
You take me in
And I am home

# Loving What Is

To love the house of fear with all its lights turned off
To love the moon above it
To love the fences and walls that we're building
To love the doors and the open spaces between us
To love those who are leaving us
To love those who are coming towards us
To love what is
Just because
It is

# Wait

Wait for the right moment
When everything aligns
Into a birth that changes everything
Yet goes unnoticed by most
That's how it's supposed to be

Lift your eyes from this page
Look at her
Even if there is no way you can ever see her
Smile and she will answer you
Watch for the playful glints of light
On the surface of the lake

Let the dance continue
Your inaudible laughter
Will make the heron fly
Fly and return

# It's not what it looks like

Even as we are silenced
Our songs reverberate
Love never ends

# The destination

Because we cannot find love
We become it

We are the children
Of our own hopes

We are the One
Who has our back

Who blows us into life after life
Like butterflies

We are the flight home

# Arrivals

You arrive on a path not in a place

This is also a departure
The path leading you wherever it will

After all these turns and twists
Trials and errors and attempts
To create something worth keeping
All there is left is the receiving and the letting go

And for some reason
That you cannot put in words
It fills your heart
Your eyes with tears
And you smile
And you move on

# It is happening

As I dance with life
Every step
Is a song of love

# Words

Let me not stop there
Let me go further
Let me go
To that meeting place
Where everything falls
Silent
Into place
Where I fall
In love
With everything
Where I lose myself
For good
Where joy lives
Where I find myself

# The answer

I am the answer
To all my questions
One by one
My questions are being answered
Moment by moment
I disappear

# Dying

Tomorrow as today
This love
Is yours as it is ours
This is the truth
It cannot die

# The cup

Removing ourselves
From ourselves

Drinking from the cup
Until there is nothing left
But a smile

# The agreement

My heart
Soft as it may be
Wants to push the limits of my chest
Bigger wider
Wants to sing its joy to the entire world
Give its gifts wherever it goes
For no reason
No holding back
My heart
Wants to bring itself to everyone
To fill their hands, their hearts, their eyes
My heart
Is impatiently waiting for me
To agree

# My soul

Even the smallest of your gifts
Is more than a world for me

Oh to take you in
Like the dried-out soil takes in the first rain

Or is it you taking me in?

# I am love

I am love
Unlike everything else
I am real
Everything else
Fears demands accusations
Regrets hurt disappointments
Oh the disappointments
All those are but temporary hindrances
To my reality
    I am love
        Entering an old house
I am the eternal breath
Breaking through windows that haven't been opened
For too long
Whipping through the abandoned stairs and cellars
    You see a tiny light through a keyhole
    But I blow the door open
    You see sleeping bodies
    But I permeate every fiber
    Every mind and heart

I am love
Illuminating the stories
And the black and white illustrations
In stacks of outdated newspapers
    I love it all
    And I won't rest
    Until I fill it all
Rejoice
Orderly times are gone
    I am unruly
    I will withhold nothing of my loving nature
    I will break through any barrier
    I will take into possession
    Everything
    Because it has been mine
    All along
It's time
To stop pretending
Enough already
The switch is on
And there is no turning it off
I am love
And this
This is just the beginning

# Thank you

There is something
That I want to say
But cannot

This is my last chance to say it
Because

Today is the last day of my life
(as is every day)

The ocean behind my eyes and heart
Has no words

    Maybe just say
    What can be said

# Gratitude

Thank you for being here, dear Reader! These poems exist only because you read them, experience them in your own way, let them inspire you. For that I thank you with all my heart.

"Love Songs" have become what you see here through the invaluable help of poetry mentor, Frances Bryant-Scott. I am so grateful for the way Franny supported me so that each poem could mature into its best expression. It was an eye-opening and inspiring journey and I feel immensely blessed to have had Franny by my side. Let her inspire you as well at Instagram.com/thread_language

A special thank you to Steinar and Eva Andrea for welcoming these poems the way you did, and for blessing me and the birth of this book with your generous love, time and ideas. It made a big difference. Eva Ditlefsen offers her magical writing at EvaAndrea.com
Steinar Ditlefsen is the founder of European Transformational Teachers Gathering. More about his extraordinary work at SteinarDitlefsen.com

Thank you, Laura Cassini, for letting me use your painting, "Blue Life", as the background for this book. It couldn't be more perfect. I am a big fan of Laura's art. She is a chromatic poetess, a sensitive artist who brings to her creations a strong, deep sense of aliveness. Her artistic work generates an immediate, intimate and unique relationship with the viewer. Experience more of her wonderful creations at ArtMajeur.com/lcasini

Thank you, JuneDesign.fr for designing a cover that reflects the poems so beautifully, in every sense of the word. I loved working with you on this project.

# About the author

My spiritual journey began when I began (that's how it works for all of us I believe), but more consciously from age 18 (which is a long time ago). Throughout the entire journey I have been drawn to attempting the impossible: expressing that which cannot be expressed.

I began with meditation and exploring the work of various spiritual teachers. My own expression emerged gradually through my music and journaling. When I reached my 30s I began to coach, mentor, and teach in various forms. In my 60s, it all came together in the *Awakening To Joyful* Living work. You can experience my body of work at HalinaGold.com.

In recent years, the calling to write has grown persistently and wonderfully stronger, and I look forward to sharing more poetry, stories, and spiritual non-fiction with you in the future.

Let's stay in touch at HalinaGold.com/books

# Other books by Halina

**Finding Joy Every Day**
*A simple daily practice for joyful living*

**Meditations for the Living**
*Turning Loneliness to Love*

**From Lonely To Home**
*A Workbook for Finding Your Way*

**Magic and Miracles**
*21 Real Life Experiences
from the Edges of Logic and Science*
(contributing author)

Lightning Source UK Ltd.
Milton Keynes UK
UKHW011310171221
395825UK00002B/302